3.0

CHILDREN'S ROOM

First Ladies

Mary Todd Lincoln

j 92 Lincoln,M STR

Launch!
An Imprint of Abdo Zoom
abdopublishing.com

Jennifer Strand

abdopublishing.com

Published by Abdo Zoom, a division of ABDO, PO Box 398166, Minneapolis, Minnesota 55439.
Copyright © 2019 by Abdo Consulting Group, Inc. International copyrights reserved in all countries.
No part of this book may be reproduced in any form without written permission from the publisher.
Launch!™ is a trademark and logo of Abdo Zoom.

Printed in the United States of America, North Mankato, Minnesota.

052018
092018

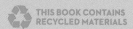

Photo Credits: Alamy, AP Images, Getty Images, Granger Collection, iStock, Shutterstock

Production Contributors: Kenny Abdo, Jennie Forsberg, Grace Hansen, John Hansen

Design Contributors: Dorothy Toth, Neil Klinepier

Library of Congress Control Number: 2017917551

Publisher's Cataloging-in-Publication Data

Names: Strand, Jennifer, author.

Title: Mary Todd Lincoln / by Jennifer Strand.

Description: Minneapolis, Minnesota : Abdo Zoom, 2019. | Series: First ladies |
Includes online resources and index.

Identifiers: ISBN 9781532122859 (lib.bdg.) | ISBN 9781532123832 (ebook) |
ISBN 9781532124327 (Read-to-me ebook)

Subjects: LCSH: Lincoln, Mary Todd, 1818-1882, Biography--Juvenile literature. | Presidents' spouses--
United States--Biography--Juvenile literature. | First ladies (United States)--Biography--Juvenile
literature.

Classification: DDC 973.70924 [B]--dc23

Table of Contents

Mary Todd Lincoln

Mary Todd Lincoln was a First Lady of the United States. Her husband Abraham Lincoln was the 16th US President. She is known for her strong support of the **Union** army during the **Civil War**.

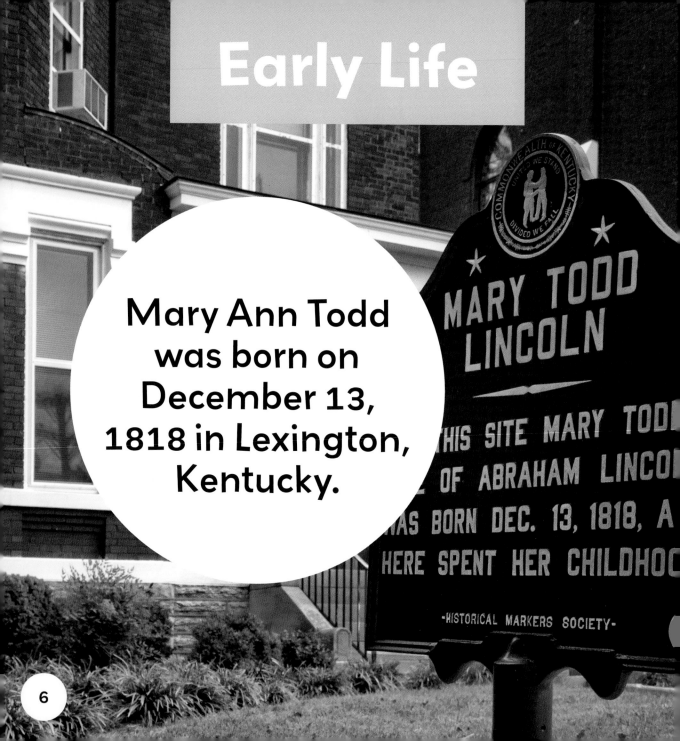

Early Life

Mary Ann Todd was born on December 13, 1818 in Lexington, Kentucky.

MARY TODD LINCOLN

THIS SITE MARY TOD OF ABRAHAM LINCO AS BORN DEC. 13, 1818, A HERE SPENT HER CHILDHOO

-HISTORICAL MARKERS SOCIETY-

Mary's father was a
successful businessman.
Their family was very **wealthy**.

She was well-educated for a woman of that time.

In 1839, Mary moved to Illinois. There, she met Abraham Lincoln. They were married in 1842 and had four children.

Leader

Mary was a strong supporter of her husband.

She would help him by hosting events and offering advice.

Mary took care of their home while Lincoln continued his job.

Mary went with Lincoln to Washington D.C. when he won his seat in **Congress**. That was new for the time.

First Lady

Mary Todd Lincoln was First Lady from 1861 to 1865.

As the First Lady, she would visit hospitals. There, she spent time with hurt soldiers.

Mary wrote letters for the soldiers. She would also visit **battlefields** with Lincoln.

Legacy

Mary spent her later years traveling through **Europe**. She returned to Illinois in 1881.

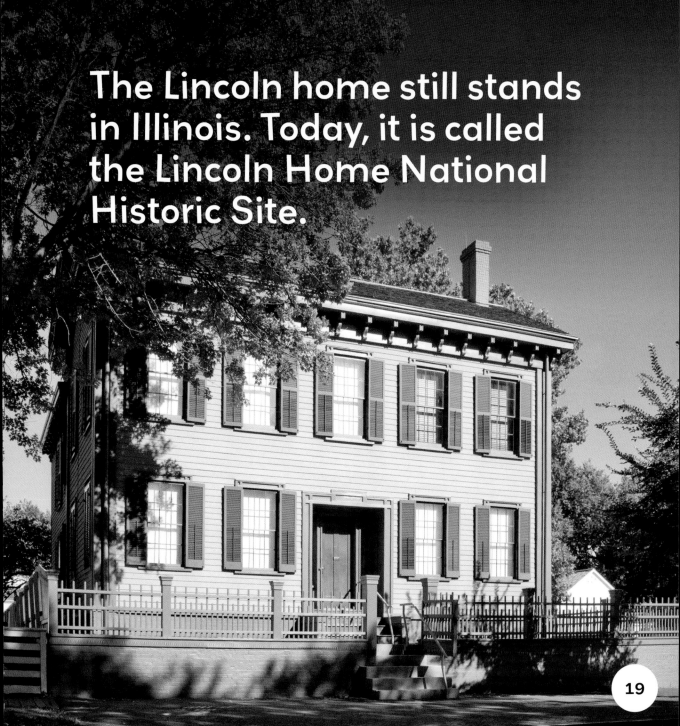

The Lincoln home still stands in Illinois. Today, it is called the Lincoln Home National Historic Site.

Mary Todd Lincoln

Born: December 13, 1818

Birthplace: Lexington, Kentucky

Husband: Abraham Lincoln

Years Served: 1861-1865

Political Party: Republican

Known For: Lincoln was a First Lady of the United States. She supported the Union Army during the Civil War.

Key Dates

1818: Mary Ann Todd is born on December 13.

1842: Mary Todd marries Abraham Lincoln on November 4.

1861-1865: Mary Todd Lincoln is the First Lady. Abraham Lincoln is the 16th president.

1876-1881: Mary lives abroad in Europe.

1882: Mary Todd Lincoln dies on July 16.

Glossary

battlefield – the ground where a battle is fought.

Civil War – a war between groups in the same country. The United States of America and the Confederate States of America fought a civil war from 1861 to 1865.

Congress – the body that makes the laws for the United States. It includes the House of Representatives and the Senate.

Europe – the continent between Asia and the Atlantic Ocean. England, France, and Italy are some of the countries in Europe.

Union – known as the North during the Civil War. They were against slavery.

wealthy – to have a lot of money.

Online Resources

For more information on
Mary Todd Lincoln, please visit
abdobooklinks.com

Learn even more with the
Abdo Zoom Biographies database.
Visit **abdozoom.com** today!

Index